JOSÉ!

Born to Dance
the story of josé limón

Susanna Reich

Illustrated by **Raúl Colón**

A PAULA WISEMAN BOOK
SIMON & SCHUSTER BOOKS FOR YOUNG READERS
New York   London   Toronto   Sydney

To Gary, *mi mejor amigo grandioso y magnífico*
—S. R.

For Dorita
—R. C.

Glossary

adiós: good-bye
carmesí: crimson; bright red
corrida de toros: bullfight ring
La danza séra mi vida: Dance will be my life
liberación: liberation
molinillo: a carved wooden whisk used to whip hot chocolate
olé: an expression of enthusiastic approval
O, soñador: Oh, dreamer
radiante: radiant; shining
sí: yes
torero: bullfighter
un artista grandioso y magnífico: a great and magnificent artist
¡Uno! ¡Dos! ¡Uno! ¡Dos!: One! Two! One! Two!

SIMON & SCHUSTER BOOKS FOR YOUNG READERS
An imprint of Simon & Schuster Children's Publishing Division
1230 Avenue of the Americas, New York, New York 10020
Text copyright © 2005 by Susanna Reich
Illustrations copyright © 2005 by Raúl Colón
SIMON & SCHUSTER BOOKS FOR YOUNG READERS is a trademark of Simon & Schuster, Inc.
Book design by Daniel Roode
The text for this book is set in Cantoria.
The illustrations for this book are rendered in watercolor and colored pencil on paper.
Manufactured in the United States of America
2 4 6 8 10 9 7 5 3 1
Library of Congress Cataloging-in-Publication Data
Reich, Susanna.
José! born to dance: the story of José Limón / Susanna Reich ; illustrated by Raúl Colón.
p. cm.
"A Paula Wiseman book."
ISBN 0-689-86576-7
1. Limón, José—Juvenile literature. 2. Dancers—United States—Biography—
Juvenile literature. 3. Choreographers—United States—Biography—Juvenile literature.
I. Colón, Raúl, ill. II. Title.
GV1785.L515R45 2005
792.8'092—dc22
2004004776

In 1908 a baby boy was born in Culiacán, Mexico,
kicking like a roped steer.
BAM!
BAM! BAM!
His name was José Limón.

When José was a toddler, Mama used to take him to
his grandmother's house for breakfast.
The pet canary sang to him while he ate.
TRILLIA-WEET! TRILLIA-WEET!
Surrounded by flowers, José feasted on mango and
papaya, pineapple and banana, sweet rolls and eggs.
His mouth watered as Grandmother whisked the hot
chocolate with her *molinillo*.
When the hot chocolate was cool enough to drink,
José gulped it down.

Sometimes Papa took José to the theater where Papa worked as a musician.

José loved to watch the dancers on the stage.

The cancan dancers lifted their petticoats and kicked their legs.

OH LA LA!

The flamenco dancers flipped their skirts and clicked their heels.

¡Sí! ¡Sí! ¡Sí!

The ballet dancers leapt into the air.

Raising their arms high above their heads, they seemed to fly.

AHHHHH!

One afternoon Papa took José to the *corrida de toros*.
In the bullfight ring a *torero* swirled his red cloak
to anger the black bull.
¡Olé! ¡Olé! ¡Olé!
The bull pawed the ground.
It ran straight toward the bullfighter, its head down
and its eyes ablaze.
José gripped Papa's hand.

Later that night, when Mama tucked José into bed,
her sweet voice echoed in the darkness.
SOBA-SOBA-SO, SOBA-SO.
That night José dreamed of the bullfight.

One spring day when José was five, he saw government
soldiers marching in the street.
A civil war had broken out in Mexico.
José slung a stick over his shoulder and marched
through the house.
¡Uno! ¡Dos! ¡Uno! ¡Dos!
The next day at breakfast, shots rang out.
The rebels had attacked their town.
Surrounded by fighting, José's family hid in the cellar
for three days and three nights.

Months passed and the war raged on.
Safety lay across the border—in the United States.
Perhaps Papa could find a job there.
José's family took a train to Nogales, close to the border.
Soldiers sat on top of the train, their guns at the ready.
The train crawled through the hot desert.
As the sun set, José heard the sound of an accordion—
a slow, mournful song.
"O, soñador . . ."

For two years José and his family lived in Nogales,
waiting and waiting for permission to enter the
United States.
Finally Papa's work permit arrived, stamped with an
official seal.
They packed their bags and set out across the
northern frontier.
Adiós, Mexico.

At José's new school the children gathered around the
teacher to read aloud from their books.
When José read, the other children laughed at his
poor English.
At first José cried.
Then he stamped his foot in fierce determination.
ᴘᴜᴍ!
I will learn this language better than any of you, he said
to himself—though it seemed nearly impossible.

But within three years José could speak English with confidence.
He was quick to learn new words and translated for Mama wherever they went.
Carmesí. Radiante. Liberación.
Crimson. Radiant. Liberation.

By sixth grade José had become known for his colorful drawings.
Among his many younger brothers and sisters he was famous for his pictures of trains.
Everyone thought he would become an artist.
But José loved music, too.
As a teenager he practiced the piano at all hours of the day and night.
When his fingers flew, his spirit soared.
AHH!

After José finished high school in Los Angeles,
Mama became very sick.
When she died, sadness lay on José's heart.
He went to work in a factory.
All day long he took tiles from one wheelbarrow and
loaded them into another.
At night he dreamed of painting and drawing.
He dreamed of living in New York, among the artists.
But he didn't know if Papa could manage without him.

José waited, and brooded, and argued with himself.
Finally, after a year, he made up his mind.
"Papa," he announced, "I'm going."
Adiós, José. Farewell.

He headed east across the continent, two thousand four hundred and sixty-two miles.

When José reached New York, the shimmering city towered above him: marble, stone, brick, and steel.
José floated down the sidewalk.
He would become a great artist, *un artista grandioso y magnífico.*
He would fill his sketchbooks with drawings like none the world had ever seen.

He took a job as a janitor, scooping ashes out of a coal furnace and hauling garbage cans to the curb.
But as winter wore on, a cold loneliness settled over José.
He missed his family, far away in sunny California.

Discouraged, he wandered the halls of the great museums.
Manet, Renoir, and Picasso, he thought.
Perhaps they had already painted everything.
His drawings would never compare.
The music in his heart fell silent.

"New York is a cemetery," he said. "A jungle of stone."
José put away his drawings.
He felt sad and lost.
How could he be an artist without an art?
He wanted to give a gift to the world, but he didn't know what it could be.

One day José's friend Charlotte invited him to a dance concert.

The dancer twisted his body and leapt into the air.

AIEEEEE!

The dance lit a fire in José's soul.

Ideas exploded in his mind.

"I do not want to remain on this earth unless I can learn to do what this man is doing!" he said.

A few days later, José stepped into a dance studio for the first time.

As soon as the pianist began to play, the sound of the music carried José away.

He swooped. He stretched. He swirled. And then he flew—

AHHHHH!

¡La danza séra mi vida!

I embrace the dance!

From then on, José took classes from teachers Doris Humphrey and Charles Weidman nearly every day.

Dripping with sweat, he struggled with his stiff and stubborn body.

And at night he hobbled home, his muscles sore and aching.

Six weeks later, he made his debut, performing for the first time.

As he waited to go onstage, he felt shy and nervous. All those people in the audience would be watching him. But once he heard the thundering applause, his spirits lifted.

"That night I tasted undreamed-of exaltation, humility, and triumph," he said.

Ankles and feet, knees and hips, chest and arms, head and neck, up and down and back and forth and in and out, José Limón wove himself into a dancer. He became what he was born to be.

For eleven years José studied and danced with Doris and Charles.

He learned to make his muscles sing.
He learned to move his bones every which way.
He learned to flow and float and fly through space with steps smooth as silk.

He learned to be fierce like a bullfighter—*¡Olé!*
Strong like a soldier—*¡Uno! ¡Dos! ¡Uno! ¡Dos!*
And proud like a king—PUM!

He learned to make dances sweet as birdsong—
TRILLIA-WEET!
Hot as the desert sun—*¡Sí! ¡Sí!*
Sad as broken dreams—*O, soñador* . . .
Loving as a mother's lullaby floating on a Mexican breeze—SORA-SORA-SO, SORA-SO.

In time José became a world-famous choreographer
and toured the globe with his own dance company.
For forty years, with bare feet and broad shoulders, he
graced the concert stage.
From New York to Mexico City and London to Buenos
Aires, he danced for presidents and princesses,
builders and bricklayers, bankers and bus drivers,
fiddlers and firemen.
And each night before the curtain rose, he whispered
to himself, "Make me strong so I can give."

BRAVO! BRAVO! BRAVO!

Historical Note

One of the great dancers and choreographers of the twentieth century, José Limón (1908–1972) was born to a family of mixed European and Native Mexican descent, the first of eleven children. After the outbreak of the Mexican Revolution, José's father lost his job as director of the State Academy of Music in Cananea, Sonora. Two years later, the Limóns moved to Tucson, Arizona, and later to Los Angeles, where José attended high school and his artistic talent blossomed.

After his mother's death, José was torn between his commitment to his family and his future as an artist. In 1928 he set out for New York City. He enrolled at the Art Students League, but—homesick, lonely, and still grieving for his mother—he soon became discouraged and left school. In February 1929 he saw a performance by the German dancer Harald Kreutzberg, and his life took a new direction.

José started taking classes with Doris Humphrey and Charles Weidman, who, along with their contemporary Martha Graham, were pioneers of the new art form of modern dance. Soon José was performing with the Humphrey-Weidman Company and in Broadway shows. In 1941 he married Pauline Lawrence, a musician and costume designer who managed the Humphrey-Weidman Company. After serving in the U.S. army during World War II, José returned to New York to start his own dance company.

In the decades that followed, José performed in works created for his company by Doris Humphrey, as well as in dances of his own. Some were rooted in his Mexican childhood, while others were inspired by Greek myths, Shakespearean tragedies, or biblical stories. Among his greatest roles were the Bullfighter in *Lament for Ignacio Sanchez Mejías* and the Moor in *The Moor's Pavane*.

Since José's death in 1972, the Limón Dance Company has continued to tour worldwide to great acclaim. José's dances have been performed by the American Ballet Theater, the Alvin Ailey American Dance Theater, the Joffrey Ballet, and many other companies. As a teacher at the Juilliard School, José inspired several generations of young dancers. The Limón dance technique, known for its dynamic rhythms and lyrical phrasing, is still taught at schools and universities around the world. In 2000 the Dance Heritage Coalition named José Limón one of "America's Irreplaceable Dance Treasures."

Bibliography

Books and Articles
Limón, José. *José Limón: An Unfinished Memoir*. Lynn Garafola, editor. Hanover, NH: Wesleyan University Press/University Press of New England, 1999.
Pollack, Barbara, and Charles Humphrey Woodford. *Dance Is a Moment: A Portrait of José Limón in Words and Pictures*. Pennington, NJ: Princeton Book Company, 1993.

Film and Video
José Limón: Three Modern Dance Classics—The Moor's Pavane, The Traitor, The Emperor Jones. Pleasantville, NY: Video Artists International, 1999.
Limón: A Life Beyond Words. Produced by Ann Vachon and Jeffrey Levy-Hinte. Directed by Malachi Roth.

Web Site
www.limon.org

The author would like to thank Ann Vachon for the loan of videotaped interviews made during the production of the film *Limón: A Life Beyond Words*. Thanks also go to Norton Owen of the José Limón Dance Foundation for his invaluable assistance during the course of research.